SMASH THE BOX!

Chad J. Willett

First Printing: 2015
Third Edition

ISBN 978-1-57074-184-5

Edited by Leonard Hayhurst and Andrea Clute

Front and Back Cover Design by Aaron Buckley

Printed in the United States of America

Published by
Braughler Books LLC
braughlerbooks.com

This book is dedicated to my family and my amazing wife.

TABLE OF CONTENTS

Read Out of Order and Smash the Box!

INTRODUCTION:

I met with my editor, Leonard Hayhurst, at Pizza Cottage in Zanesville, Ohio, about the idea of writing a book. I went into the meeting thinking I was going to eat some pizza, drink some Mountain Dew, and leave without really writing anything. However, I kept an open mind. I told myself if I felt a book were a possibility after meeting with Leonard, then I would write it, but if not, that would be okay, too.

The only reason I ever thought of writing a book is because I am a motivational speaker. Any speaker who is "making it" writes a book, so that was my catalyst. I definitely had a negative view of the process, in part, because everyone writes books nowadays, and I didn't want to be one of those "people." To be honest, the idea of writing something that no one would read or find interesting didn't really excite me.

I went into this meeting with a completely open mind, which was a shift for me. I generally go into meetings wanting to present my ideas, control the conversation and dictate the results — all of which are qualities of being "in the box." For some reason, I was completely open during this meeting and whatever the outcome, I was going to be okay with it. In short, I gave up control when I met with Leonard, and the result was very surprising.

As I put another piece of pizza in my mouth, Leonard made a great point. He said, "Books can be short, like under a hundred pages." For some reason, this really hit home for me and made me think of a book that had a profound impact on my life, a very small book called *The Four Agreements*. The paperback is a little over a hundred pages and a very simple read.

Leonard eased my mind on how long a book HAS TO BE and this made me feel a little better about the process.

He went on to tell me all I need to do is tell the stories about "SMASH THE BOX" and let the readers learn from my experiences. "Your audience can learn through the stories you share, and that should be the vehicle through which you write the book, rather than telling them how to be creative or think outside the box."

As I sipped on some more Mountain Dew, we had a moment. I turned to Leonard and told him I didn't want this to be like all other self-help books that included blank pages, activities, and the like. This didn't excite me. I told him I would like to "ruin the take" on this book. Leonard, with a piece of pepperoni sticking out of his mouth, gave me a quizzical look as he wondered what the heck "ruin the take" was. I explained the concept to him, which we will get into in the SMASH portion of the book.

And then the magic happened. Leonard said, "Let's "SMASH THE BOOK." The concept of how a book has to be written: table of contents, linear, page-numbered, front cover, back cover, positive testimonials, subtitles and the rest didn't have to be followed verbatim. The process of how people have been written for hundreds of years is a box in and of itself. We have **SMASHED THE BOOK! Enjoy!**

BROWN BEAR

BROWN BEAR

My mom and I decided that each summer we wanted to "Smash the Box" and do something completely different. We wanted to do something out of our comfort zone and off the script of life — in short, we wanted to improvise. We told ourselves that we would be open to new adventures, possibilities, and do things outside of our normal, everyday life. Two summers ago, we "Smashed the Box" by visiting one of her friends who lived out in the country in Zanesville, Ohio. Zanesville is 60 miles east of Columbus, in the foothills of the Appalachian Mountains.

We drove out to her friend's house tucked away in the woods. This house was off the grid. It was surrounded by woods, dirt roads, and wild animals. I adjusted my sunglasses as I got out of the car and saw a cement cage on the side of the home. I noticed something moving around in the pen.

I wondered what in the world a huge cage was doing on the side of this woman's house, but I didn't judge it. I followed my mom up the driveway. As we got closer to the cage, I noticed that the creature inside was brown, furry, and had a black snout. I couldn't believe my eyes; it was a bear. I had seen bears at the zoo, but I had never seen a brown bear face-to-face ever in my life.

Next, we met my mother's friend as she walked down the driveway, and the first thing out of my mom's mouth was, "Chad, do you want to go in the cage with the bear?" My initial response was "no" — and not just "no" but with an "are you kidding me?" connotation. No, I don't want to get in a cage with a brown bear! I had a flood of thoughts going through my head such as being eaten by this bear, getting trapped in the cage, and having my face ripped apart by this wild beast.

But, I remembered the "Yes And" technique from my days training as an actor and I softly said "yes" as I followed her up to the cage. As we were waiting on the owner to get the key to unlock the cage, I looked inside and saw this amazing brown bear. It was about a year and a half old and close to 200 pounds with lush fur, a brown snout, and piercing brown eyes.

This giant predator was playing on the top level of the cage as we were watching it from afar. It was on its back, rubbing its fur up against the wooden planks of the cage on this sun-filled day without a care in the world. It knew we were there watching it, yet it was in its own little world.

The lady returned with her husband, and he unlocked the cage. I found it interesting that the husband came with the wife as we all entered the cage; it told me that we needed reinforcements on this excursion. As we slowly entered the cage, my heart started beating faster and my hands became cold. I didn't have time to think; it all happened so fast. Before I knew it, I was face to face with the bear in its cement cage.

Once in the cage, I was trying to keep my distance from it, but sure enough, it found its way to me and the group within seconds. The moment we unlocked the gate, he made his way down to check us out as we entered his domain. Within 30 seconds, he came up to me and rubbed his head on my leg. As he passed me and went to check out the others, I petted his back and registered how soft his fur was. I thought about how this was a once-in-a-lifetime experience as I rubbed my hands through the wild animal's fur.

After the bear checked us out, he made his way back up onto the first platform and sat down. He looked at the four of us in the cage one by one with piercing brown eyes and the slightest of grins. There was no doubt we were in this bear's territory, and he was letting us know that.

We stayed in the cage a few minutes. The bear gave us a look that he wanted to play, but he didn't have any takers. I was the first one to exit the cage, followed by the owners, and then my mom. I looked back as I exited the cage to a sight I will never forget.

The bear grabbed my mom's hair with its paw as she was starting to leave and then put both paws over her head. Seeing my mom's head buried between the bear's paws was one of the scariest sights I had ever seen. The owner rushed back into the cage yelling at the bear to let go of my mom's hair. The bear scurried off onto the second platform, and the owner helped my mom get out of the cage.

My mother was bent over with her hair disheveled once out of the cage. I went to her side and asked whether she was okay. Raising her head with a big smile, she said, "Yes, the bear was just playing with my hair and I am fine." I exhaled, recovered from my mini-heart attack, and said a quick prayer thanking the Lord that my mom was okay.

This was one of the scariest, most exciting, and craziest things I have done in my life and I loved it. The memory of being in a cage with a brown bear will be with me forever and, more importantly, it's a memory I can share with my mom. That is what "Smashing the Box" is all about; it is getting off the script of life and improvising. It's doing the unplanned and the unexpected. It's about taking a leap of faith.

As you read this book, my hope is that you have your own "Brown Bear" moment — a moment where you take a leap of faith, get off the script of life and try something new, exciting, and different. However, I don't recommend getting in a cage with a wild animal.

The brown bear was a rescued animal in Zanesville. The owners are seeking a permanent location for the bear to spend the remainder of its life.

MENTAL PRISON

INTRODUCTION

Smash the Box is a handbook, a guide to help readers become more creative. I purposefully wrote this book not as a step-by-step manual on how to be more creative, but rather as an opportunity for the reader to learn from stories where I was a prisoner in the "Mental Prison" and the times I escaped. There is no simple answer on how to be more creative. However, if you are aware of the walls you create and use the techniques discussed in this book, you will have an opportunity to think and act outside the box. The stories you will read are from my days in Los Angeles and Columbus, with acting being the thread that binds them. You will discover the four walls of the "Mental Prison," how to "Smash the Box," and what it is like to live inside and outside of the "Mental Prison."

WHAT IS THE BOX?

I find it interesting that everyone uses the phrase "think outside the box," without defining what the *box* is. What are we trying to escape — what *is* the box? I have defined the box as when we are thinking, living, and operating out of our head, a state that I label the "Mental Prison." When we are in our head, we are prisoners to our mind and not in the present moment. We are not at liberty to be spontaneous, free, or creative. The box is when we are in our head and a prisoner to our mind.

MENTAL PRISON

The "Mental Prison" is when we are trapped in our head, reflecting on the past or thinking about the future. We are basically not in the moment listening, reacting, and operating off of the environment around us. The "Mental Prison" isn't meant to be a negative term, but a symbol that represents our inability to produce ideas, thoughts, or actions outside the conventional way of thinking.

I also use the term *Mental Prison* to paint a picture in your mind. We often imagine prisons to be dark, gray, restricted, and contained. It's the opposite of creativity. The "Mental Prison" represents uniformity, rigidity, control, and fear.

WE CREATE THE WALLS

When we are trapped in our head, we are in the "Mental Prison." This prison has four distinct walls that keep us captive. The four walls I write about are broad in nature, but can have a life-long stranglehold on our creative capabilities if we aren't aware of them or combat them. The more we build these walls, the harder it is for us to innovate, create, and connect.

The four walls of the "Mental Prison" are:

1. Perfection
2. Negativity
3. Judgment
4. Fear

The "Mental Prison" wants us to be self-absorbed, introspective, and cut off from the world we operate in. The more selfish we are with our time, money, and attention, the higher these walls become. Ironically, creativity is about getting the focus off of us and onto someone or something else. It's about giving, charity, and being selfless. It's about giving away our gifts and talents to others.

Creativity is tricky and elusive. Yet, simple techniques discussed in this book will be a spark to your creative capabilities and slowly break down your walls. Let us begin with the first wall of the "Mental Prison."

WALL #1

PERFECTION

Are you a perfectionist? I am. The more perfect I want things to be, the more pressure I put on myself and others. This creates the first wall of the "Mental Prison." Perfection stunts the creative process by limiting two extremely important parts of the creative process — experimentation and exploration.

In order to experiment and explore, we must make mistakes, fail, and in short, be imperfect. Any successful artist, businessman, or businesswoman who is creative has failed, made mistakes, and been imperfect. The only people who are perfect are the people who don't experiment, explore, try new things, start a new business or change their company culture. They'd rather sit on the sidelines and play it safe. This wall grows the more we demand perfection of ourselves and others, and perfectionism crushes the creative process.

Over the past three years, I have been speaking to groups, organizations, and companies about creativity, innovation, and thinking big, bold and audacious thoughts. My signature keynote address is "Smash the Box," which follows the format of this book. It's unscripted and improvised while breaking rules, patterns, and routines.

While on the road, I find it interesting to see the reactions I receive when I talk about the wall of perfection. People have a difficult time thinking they can be imperfect. I would suggest this is part of the reason why so few companies and individuals are creative. They don't experiment or explore. These two elements are a key component of the creative process, but they can also lead to mistakes and failures.

My concept of perfectionism being a wall in the creative process was put to a test in the winter of 2016. I was the breakfast keynote speaker to a homebuilder association in Des Moines, Iowa, and I presented "Smash the Box." Naturally, during the address I talked about perfection and how it kills the creative process. When I finished my talk, I sat down at the head table and the emcee came back up to the podium and began giving out awards. One of the awards he gave out was a lifetime achievement award for an architect in the Des Moines area.

During this award, they had a video tribute that lasted three minutes showing this man's designs. They were beautiful, creative, and innovative. At the end of the video, the gentleman said what made him creative and innovative was being a perfectionist. Here I am sitting at the head table where I just said perfectionism crushes the creative process, and he said that is what made him the artist he is. He went on to say that attention to detail is the key to his designs and the homes that he creates.

After this tribute ended, we took a break and a gentleman approached me and asked about this contradiction. He said, "so who is right, you or the architect regarding perfection?" I told him we both are, and he looked at me like I was a politician. I wasn't trying to con this man. I was trying to say there is room at the end of the creative process for perfection, but not in the process itself.

I told this man I know that the architect was a perfectionist on the finished product. However, during the process, he experiments and explores when working on his blueprints with drawing, sketching, and planning. Remember, architects use pencils with erasers, because they know they will be making mistakes. They will try different bricks on the house, rearrange the design of the kitchen, the layout of the garage, the position of the backyard, the stones in the driveway, the color schemes and more. The whole design process is one big experiment or, as I like to call it, a perfect mess. I can't imagine how many times this and other architects have erased, re-drawn, and re-colored their blueprints before they showcase the finished product to clients.

Yes, the finished product will be clean, simple, and perfect, but what got them to that point is imperfection. And herein lies the key — during the process, we must experiment and explore (like the architect) if we are to think and generate ideas outside the box. It is okay to be a perfectionist at the end of a project and pay attention to all the details. But we can't allow perfectionism to seep into the process, our meetings, our designs and our brainstorming sessions, or creativity will be affected.

The wall of perfection keeps us boxed in by discouraging mistakes. However, the creative process is dependent upon mistakes; the more creative one is, the more mistakes he or she will make.

WALL #2

NEGATIVITY

Generally speaking, are you a negative or positive person? (Only you know the true answer.) I see myself as a positive person, but very few people see themselves as negative. Yet, when I go to companies, they tell me that the majority of their employees are negative. Can you see the disconnect? No one thinks they are negative, yet, companies all across the USA say they have negative employees. So who is right?

As you can see, this wall is tricky. It is very hard to detect because none of us want to admit that we are negative. Of all the walls in the "Mental Prison," this is the one that always goes undetected, because very few people can look themselves in the mirror and own up to this part of themselves. To be honest, it is difficult for *me* to admit. I have my days when I am negative, and you will read about them in this section.

I have learned from being on the speaking trail for the past three years that the wall of negativity is created by what we focus on, making assumptions, and taking things personally. The power of this wall strengthens and magnifies the more we focus on ourselves, make assumptions, and think everything is about us. We manufacture our reality, whether positive or negative. This is exactly what I did while auditioning in L.A.; I created my wall of negativity.

When I acted in L.A., I was negative and my inner dialogue was toxic. I thought that I sucked as an actor, that I was not good enough, not funny, charismatic or skilled enough to land roles. These thoughts would go through my head all the way through an audition.

I recall an audition for a student film at Loyola Marymount University in L.A. You would be surprised that even for a student film of low budget and quality that doesn't pay, you are going up against a number of actors. In Los Angeles, everyone is an actor and needs work. I was auditioning for the lead in an 8-minute short film. I could credit this role on my resume and use the footage on my demo reel to help me get paying jobs.

After arriving at the audition and signing in, I waited in the lobby and began building the "Mental Prison." I thought about how I am not any good, I don't have the right look for it, I am too skinny; the negative talk went on and on. When I got called into the room, I read my lines and auditioned. The director, a student at LMU, shook his head after my audition. I was confused and just stared at him. With a depressed look on his face, he said that he wanted me to do it again.

The camera rolled a second time, and I said the lines, performed, and finished the audition. After the second take, the director came over to a chair and sat down next to me. I could tell in the tone of his voice that he really wanted me to do well and get this part. He said I had the look and physicality for what he wanted to cast in the role. However, there was one problem — my audition. He told me I needed to relax and perform less if I was to get this part. He couldn't cast me unless I was natural with my delivery.

He had me do one more take, but it was the same result. I was nervous, over-performing, and sounding unnatural. At this moment, all I wanted to do was leave the room. I know the director was a good kid and his heart was in the right place, but I couldn't give him what he wanted. Still to this day I remember the look on his face as I walked through the halls of LMU and said goodbye; it was one of disappointment. He truly wanted to cast me for this role, but my audition wasn't good enough, and part of the problem was my negative self-talk. I didn't have the confidence or belief in myself to land this role and play this character.

As I walked out of the school building, all I could think about was how my negative self-talk made me a prisoner in my mind, and I couldn't escape. Even worse, the more I tried to escape the "Mental Prison," the worse my acting became. I always struggled with confidence as an actor, and part of the issue was my negative self-talk, a bad habit I had developed during my senior year at the University of Kentucky.

In May 1997, I was a week away from graduating when my professor called me into his office for a quick meeting. He'd gotten word that I was going to move out to L.A. to begin a career in acting, and he wanted to give me some advice. As I entered his office, I could tell this was not going to be a motivational pep talk.

I sat down in a chair across from my professor, who was sitting at his desk focused completely on me. He said, "Chad, you will never be a professional actor." Here I was less than a week away from graduating in the theater program and moving to Los Angeles, and a professor is telling me I am not a good actor. This is the same man who cast me in my one main stage role at the college, in a play called *Wedding Band* — a man I looked up to and admired.

I was speechless. I couldn't believe he would say that to me; I felt like I had been hit over the head with a baseball bat. He went on to say that I would make a great producer or director, but not an actor. I didn't have the skill set to make it in many cities, especially L.A. That was it. I got up, thanked him for his time, and left his office.

Looking back at my acting career in L.A., I know this comment affected my confidence, self-esteem, and belief in myself as an actor. I wasn't mentally tough enough to use his statement as positive motivation and push myself to become a successful actor and prove him wrong even though his comments were more or less true.

Looking back on L.A., learning in the classrooms and on sets have been one of the greatest times of my life and experiences I will always cherish. I use these skills I gained there as a motivational speaker on a daily basis, and I know my time and training in L.A. was a big reason for my success as a speaker. However, my wall of negativity hindered any chances I had of landing roles and having success in L.A. as an actor.

The wall of negativity isn't just what we say to others, it is also our self-talk and inner dialogue. When we are overly critical, judgmental, and negative to ourselves, this builds the wall and keeps us captive in the "Mental Prison." Have you had someone plant seeds of negativity in you? It can be with us for years to come if we are unaware of our inner dialogue. Check out your inner dialogue on Activity Number 2.

WALL #3

FEAR

Does fear keep you from chasing your dreams, taking risks, trying new things, or doing the unimaginable? The more we succumb to fear, the fewer risks we take, the fewer challenges we accept, and the less likely we are to tap into our full creative potential. The power of this wall lies in the unknown and listening to people who have very little knowledge or experience in our dreams or aspirations, but who offer opinions anyway. These voices keep us captive in the "Mental Prison."

I taught at Los Angeles Unified School District while working as an actor. Many people told me not to teach in LAUSD and gave me multiple reasons on why not to. Keep in mind, the people offering the advice had never spent one day in LAUSD; they were relaying information they heard from others. From that information, they had a perception of the school district they believed to be true and wanted to share with me. This was a wall built of fear and not facts. I was given a list of reasons why I shouldn't be a substitute teacher in the district.

First, I was told the schools looked like a prison, and my life would be in jeopardy. Second, each school had an LAPD officer assigned to it due to the gangs and the violence. Third, many classrooms didn't have textbooks and I wouldn't teach, I would babysit. Fourth, students had to wear certain color uniforms so they wouldn't be affiliated with a particular gang. Finally, I was told the schools would be covered with gang graffiti.

I found the reality to be somewhat different. Yes, the schools did look like prisons, such as Watts Middle School where I first taught. It was in downtown L.A., near Compton, where the kids came from broken families, were exposed to violence, and had very little to no support or role models.

I drove by the school in my old Nissan Sentra the first time, because the building looked abandoned. The outside of the building had burn marks on the doors and windows. I thought there was no way they could have kids in this building. I double-checked the address I was given as I stopped at a stop sign and found that I was at the right spot.

I turned to the side of the school building, parked my car, grabbed my bag and headed into the school to see whether this was really where I was teaching. When I got to the front, I opened up the burned-out steel door and made my way into a rundown walkway to the main office, where I saw a lady behind a desk. I asked, "Is this Watts Middle School?" and the lady said, "yes, who are you subbing for?" She knew right away I was a substitute teacher and new to this area. I knew that I was in a totally different culture and environment.

The school just didn't look like a prison; it looked like a burned-down one. I couldn't believe students actually went to class in this terrible structure. In the four years I was a substitute teacher, this was the worst building I was ever in. All the schools had fences around the perimeter, but not all of them resembled prisons. There were schools that had new buildings, lush grass, and great facilities. There was a great diversity in buildings and resources from one school to the next, but the majority did have a prison look and feel to them.

Yes, schools in L.A. had LAPD officers assigned to them, including Watts Middle School. On my very first day of subbing, I met an officer in my classroom, which was completely unexpected. I was subbing for a special education class. I dropped off my bags at the desk, wrote my name on the blackboard, and waited for the kids to enter. The first person to come in was Jorge, an aide. He was a character with slicked-back jet-black hair. He came straight to my desk and introduced himself as "Mr. Jorge." He went on to say that we only had eight kids, but they can be trouble and to let him handle them. I leaned back in my chair and said, "No problem."

Only six of the eight kids showed up, with Deandre the last to arrive. Deandre didn't say hello to me or Jorge. He went straight to his chair without making eye contact with anyone. Jorge didn't like the fact that Deandre didn't say hi to us and went straight to his desk. Jorge looked him in the eye and said, "I said hi to you." Deandre got up from his desk and went toe-to-toe with Jorge. He looked him straight in the eyes without saying a word.

Jorge went on to say that if he couldn't talk to us, he was going to throw him out of the class. Deandre, still not saying a word, just stared at Jorge. Jorge broke the showdown by going to the classroom phone and calling the campus police.

Within minutes, a police officer came down and escorted Deandre out of our room and into his office. Jorge ended up doing most of the teaching that day, while all I could think about was Deandre and the police officer. There was a part of me that wanted to go down and check on Deandre; however, I didn't have the courage to do it. I subbed for more than five years and I saw police officers at all the schools, but this was the only time I had one come into the classroom.

I have a laid-back personality, and many people find it hard to believe that I could teach and control these inner-city kids. However, life has many surprises, and what I found teaching in the inner city is that everything boils down to respect. I always respected all students, and I demanded respect back. Respect, not fear, allowed me to connect with students. There were many teachers whom I saw come and go trying to scare these kids or use fear tactics that didn't work. In the end, I learned as long as I respected them and they respected me, we could create a classroom where students could learn.

One of the biggest disappointments I experienced as a substitute teacher was a lack of supplies. There were a number of classes I would go into where the kids did not have textbooks. It was unfathomable to me that kids could be in school and not have books they worked out of. How could these students do homework or anything else without a textbook?

I discovered some classrooms didn't have textbooks because kids would lose them or tear them up. Therefore, the schools used copies of textbook pages for the problem classes. As you can imagine, the rooms without textbooks were usually very chaotic and undisciplined. I truly felt like the kids in these classrooms were getting an unfair education and paying the price for being in an inner-city school system.

As for uniforms, the majority of schools had a dress code the students had to abide by. In East L.A., students wore khaki pants and white button-down shirts every day to school. The reason for the dress code was to prevent kids from wearing gang colors and inciting violence at school. The neutral colors were a way to keep the kids from promoting their gangs while in school.

I actually liked the dress code; all the kids had the same look, and I do believe it reduced violence. There were still problems and tensions throughout; however, the idea that everyone looked and dressed the same eased some of the tension felt in the schools. It also put everyone on the same playing field —

it was hard for students to out-dress one another when they all wore the same outfits.

I had an experience with graffiti at Garfield High School in East L.A. I was walking into the school's main entrance, and on the side of the building was a massive gang symbol painted all over the walls. All the walls at Garfield High School were painted in a neutral beige color on purpose, and the walls this day were bright red, orange, and green with wild symbols representing a local gang.

Generally, whenever students tagged (painted) the walls, the first thing the school would do is have their staff paint over it with the beige paint. However, on this day, the tagging must have happened early in the morning and they didn't have time to paint over the graffiti before staff and students arrived. It was a strange feeling walking by a series of graffiti letters on my way to the office and realizing the environment I was working in.

By the end of the school day, they had painted over all the graffiti. As I walked to my car, I saw two teens on the street corner getting ready to fight. There was a mob of students surrounding the kids as they were getting into it, and within minutes I heard the local police coming over to break up the fight. All I could think about as I left the school was that the graffiti on the walls and the fight that broke out after school were tied to one another. I rarely saw fights during my five years of substitute teaching; however, when I did, the environment played a major role.

I truly felt bad for these kids in the LAUSD school district and the horrible environment they had to learn in. They were disadvantaged by living in the city and receiving this type of education in an environment that resembled a prison. The majority of the kids I taught were respectful, honest, and wanted a better life. I would stay after class and talk to many students about their home life and the tough circumstances they had to deal with. I realized many of them wanted someone to listen to them and hear their story. I wish I had done more of that for them.

I am very grateful I didn't allow the wall of fear to keep me from substitute teaching. Despite some of these fears being valid, what LAUSD taught me was to be thankful for the circumstances I was brought up in. When I graduated from high school, I was arrogant and aloof to the opportunities I had been given. I believed everyone had the same educational opportunities as I had, and we were all playing on a level field.

The youth from L.A. showed me the playing field is not level and that many students do not have the same opportunities as kids who live in more affluent areas. I realized segregation is not determined by race, but by money. The more money a family has, the better an opportunity they have for a quality education.

The wall of fear keeps us "boxed" into our own little world, and if I hadn't been a substitute teacher in L.A., I would have never known this world existed. I would have gone through life thinking all kids had the same opportunity I did growing up. They were just worse off because they didn't work as hard or apply themselves like I did. I still believe in accountability, but my perception has changed when I run into kids from the inner city.

WALL #4

JUDGMENTS

Do you make snap judgments about people you come in contact with? Do you create stories about people when you first meet them, make assumptions about where they are from, how much money they make, and what they do for a living? Judgments are easy to make, and if we aren't careful, we can make hundreds and hundreds of them without being aware of it. Here is one judgment I made while waiting tables in L.A.

I was a waiter at a restaurant in Beverly Hills on the famous Rodeo Drive where many celebrities came for the star treatment. They received free food and drinks and had access to a private screening room where they could hang out with their entourage into the late hours of the night. I rarely waited on the celebrities since I was a new server and this was a privilege saved for more experienced staff.

However, on a random Tuesday night, Charlie Sheen called into the restaurant and reserved space for himself and a party of 10. The manager on duty liked me and assigned me to wait on his group. This was my first experience waiting directly on a celebrity. I started getting nervous as I made an array of judgments on what the party would be like. Within seconds, I had a list of ideas of how the night would go, and none of them relating to Sheen were good.

- He will get drunk.
- He will be difficult to deal with.
- His group will be wild.
- I am going to get out very late this night.
- He won't tip.

- I am going to regret being assigned to this group.

Can you see what I just did? I made seven snap judgments about Charlie and his group, and I hadn't even met them yet. This is what the wall of judgment does; it clouds our perception, taints our experiences, and allows us to manufacture a negative reality. I began manufacturing a negative reality about Charlie before he even arrived, and I was doing all of this in my head.

The beginning of the story in my head had Sheen showing up late with his group and ordering alcoholic drinks the minute they entered the screening room. This party was supposed to start at 7:00 p.m., and I pictured them arriving around 8:00 or 8:30 p.m. and getting drunk immediately.

The middle of the story had this group being very demanding and picky with their orders. I imagined them being rude to me as they gave their orders with very little eye contact and an attitude. It always bothered me when patrons didn't make eye contact with me as a server. I was sure they would order entrees not on the menu and specialty drinks, all of which are a nightmare to a server.

The end of my story had the group leaving around 1:00 in the morning, long past their 11 p.m. deadline. I pictured Sheen stumbling by me intoxicated, belligerent, and leaving me no tip. This would be my only table all night, as it was a rule that when waiting on a celebrity you wouldn't wait on any other parties in order to give them your full attention.

The wall of judgment made me selfish. All I was concerned about was getting out on time, making a good tip, and leaving to go to sleep. I didn't see it at the time, but the more I judged, the more selfish I became.

In addition, my judgments were not based on facts or truths, but on assumptions and a fictitious story I made up in my head. Consequently, I was in a bad mood before the group even arrived, because I was already trapped in the "Mental Prison."

The facts of the real story are much different from what I made up. Sheen arrived with his guests at 7:15 p.m. They went straight to the screening room to order drinks and get ready for their movie. Everyone drank except Sheen, who ordered a cranberry juice. I went down to the bar, got all the drinks, and brought them back up for the group. From here, they sat down, ordered their dinner, and started their movie.

Everyone quietly watched the movie and ate their food. They all ordered more alcoholic drinks, except for Sheen, who stuck with cranberry juice. Around 10:15 p.m., the movie ended and the guests slowly trickled out one by one, leaving only Charlie Sheen sitting alone in a lounge chair playing with his phone. As I was loading up a tray with dirty plates, drinks, and food, Sheen came out of his chair and approached me. He asked me where I was from. I told him I was from Ohio and that I went to college at the University of Kentucky. He smiled and went on to say that he loved Kentucky, especially the horses.

His eyes shined as he talked about horses, the Kentucky Derby, and the beautiful white picket fences found in the state. As we finished our conversation, he reached into one of his pockets and took out two bills, and handed them to me while saying "Good job tonight." I stuffed the bills in my apron, shook his hand, and watched him as he exited the room and went toward the elevators.

I looked up at the clock, and it read 11:15 p.m. All I could think was what a great group to wait on. Next, I reached into the apron and actually looked at the two crumpled-up bills Sheen had given me. They were two $100 bills. It was the biggest tip I ever received as a waiter during my time in L.A. As an actor who didn't make a lot of money, getting this tip was a big deal, and I was very grateful.

However, it wasn't the tip that mattered, it was the lesson I learned about making judgments. Every judgment I made about Charlie was incorrect:

- He will be difficult to deal with. (He was easygoing.)
- He will get drunk. (He didn't drink.)
- His group will be wild. (They were polite and calm all night.)
- I am going to get out very late this night. (They left on time and I got out early.)
- He won't tip. (Sheen tipped $200.)
- I am going to regret being assigned to this group. (It was one of my best memories living in L.A.)

The fictitious story I made up in my head prior to Sheen's arriving was all wrong. The wall of judgment causes you to not only judge people, but also to manufacture a negative reality around them. I convinced myself that I didn't want to wait on this group due to the judgments I made and the fictitious story I created in my head.

When we are not in the moment, we are in the "Mental Prison" creating false realities, believing unfounded truths, and operating from a set of stereotypes and prejudices. The wall of judgment keeps us disconnected, clouds our perceptions of people, and crushes the creative process by trapping us in the prison.

CHAPTER SUMMARY

We create our "Mental Prison" as a construct of our mind. By demanding perfection, focusing on the negatives, fearing the unknown, and making judgments, we create the walls that keep us captive. What is your biggest wall? (See Activity Number 1.)

1. Perfection
2. Negativity
3. Judgment
4. Fear

In closing, imagine a life where you allow yourself to make mistakes, focus on the positives, judgment is suspended, and fear is not a factor. In short, a life lived outside the box.

Activity #1

What Is Your Biggest Wall?

Answer these questions with a simple "yes" or "no" answer. Do not over-think or over-analyze the question. Simply read it, answer it, and move on to the next question.

Question #1:

Do you desire perfection out of yourself?

Question #2:

Do you accept that others are not perfect?

Question # 3:

Do you accept your mistakes as part of the learning process?

Question #4:

Do you get upset when others make mistakes?

Question #5:

Do you like to experiment and explore?

Question #6:

Do you look for what is good in every person you interact with?

Question #7:

Do you like to complain?

Question #8:

Do you like to gossip about others?

Question #9:

Do you dwell on problems?

Question #10:

Do you beat yourself up for mistakes?

Question #11:

Do you enjoy going to new places, exploring the world, and moving away from your family?

Question #12:

Are you uncomfortable in a new environment?

Question #13:

Is your comfort zone the safest place for you to live and achieve?

Question #14:

Do you say "No" more than "Yes" when presented with new opportunities?

Question #15:

Do you like change and for things to not stay the same?

Question #16:

Do you make snap judgments on people when you meet them?

Question #17:

Do you create stories in your head that have a beginning, middle, and end before the events have happened?

Question #18:

Do people from different backgrounds make you uncomfortable?

Question #19:

When you meet someone, do you immediately put a story with them?

Question #20:

Are you constantly thinking about the past and the future, and not living in the present?

Test Results:

Add up your scores:

Total Number of "Yes" responses:

Total Number of "No" responses:

Questions #1–5/**Wall of Perfection**/Total Number of "Yes" in the first 5 questions: _____

Questions #6–10/**Wall of Negativity**/Total Number of "Yes" in questions 6–10:_____

Questions #11–15/**Wall of Fear**/Total Number of "Yes" in questions 11–15:_____

Questions #16–20/**Wall of Judgment**/Number of "Yes" in questions 16–20:_____

What is your highest number of "Yes" responses, and what group is it in?_____

That is the largest wall in your "Mental Prison."

*Ron Matias, PhD: Psychological Counseling and Testing

Activity #2

Stream-of-Consciousness Technique

The stream-of-consciousness technique comes from the world of acting, and it taps into our subconscious mind. In order to do this activity, you will need the following supplies:

- Pen or pencil
- Four blank sheets of paper
- Quiet space
- Stopwatch or timer

Below are four prompts. Read each prompt, and on your sheet of paper write whatever comes to your mind. Do each prompt separately from one another while allowing 90 seconds for each prompt.

The key is to not censor or judge what you are writing. There is no right or wrong answer. Just write freely, honestly, and candidly. The more honest and candid you are with yourself, the more you will get out of this exercise.

Your prompts are below.

Stream-of-Consciousness Prompt #1:

You and perfection — Start writing

Stream-of-Consciousness Prompt #2:

You and negativity — Start writing

Stream-of-Consciousness Prompt #3:

You and fear — Start writing

Stream-of-Consciousness Prompt #4:

You and judgment— Start writing

SMASH

THE

BOX

SMASH THE BOX

Smash the Box is about improvising, getting off the script of life, and creating. If you remember one thing from this book, remember this — in order to "Smash the Box," we must improvise to escape the "Mental Prison." The idea of being free, uninhibited, and spontaneous is everything opposite of a prison. *Smash the Box* focuses on four techniques I learned while training at The Groundlings School of Improvisation in Hollywood. They are:

1. Get the Focus Off of You
2. Embrace Mistakes
3. Say "Yes And"
4. Make Statements

The Groundlings is a school that teaches the art of improvisation, or thinking on your feet and creating as an actor without a script. Many cast members from "Saturday Night Live" come from this school. Again, there is no manual or step-by-step process to be more creative. It is a mindset we must embrace if we are to enter this state. If you want to "Smash the Box," here is how.

TECHNIQUE #1

GET THE FOCUS OFF OF YOU

The Groundlings taught us to get the focus off of us and onto someone or something else. When our focus is on ourselves, we are in prison thinking about the past, anticipating the future, and not in the present moment. There is nothing wrong with introspection, but at that moment we are not in a creative space. Spontaneity, a key to the art of improvisation, requires us to be in the moment and present.

I had a firsthand experience with a master craftsman on getting the focus off of you, improvising, and being in the present moment when Brian, owner of a wireless security company, in Columbus, Ohio, hired me to be his acting coach. He wanted to film a 3-minute infomercial to put on his security company's website. The cast included Brian, a local L.A. actor named Allen, and William Shatner, the iconic Captain Kirk from *Star Trek*.

The owner of this company was a character, to say the least. He was outgoing, bombastic, witty, and completely off the wall. Of all the students I have ever worked with, this man took the cake for being the biggest character.

When I was working with him at the studio, it was impossible to keep his attention, and being in a music room didn't help. I would start coaching him on his script, and he would jump over to the drum set during our conversation and begin drumming. He would tell me to go on with my teaching as he was drumming away a song from the rock band Journey. From here, he would jump to the piano and then check his cell phone while only occasionally sitting down and doing the scene we were working on. Needless to say, this was the most challenging and frustrating, yet entertaining, six weeks of my acting teaching career.

We flew out to L.A. the day before the shoot and had a read-through on Wednesday night, with the infomercial shoot scheduled on Thursday morning. On the day of the shoot, I was on the sound stage with Brian, William Shatner, Allen, and the production crew. If you have never been on a sound stage, there are three cameras: one stage left, one in the center, and one stage right. I was buried in the corner of the stage right behind the camera operator along with some production assistants.

Watching Shatner act was awesome. He was in the moment with improvisation while also being totally aware of his environment. One of the camera operators moved his camera a couple of feet to the left to change his angle. When Shatner finished a conversation with Brian on set, he slowly walked over to the camera operator and whispered, "Move your camera back two feet." Then he resumed the shoot.

The camera operator looked confused, thinking how in the world did he know that he moved his camera two feet in between the takes? And more importantly, why did Shatner care? The only reason I heard this conversation take place is that I was buried behind this particular camera operator.

When Brian ended the shoot, the first thing I asked him was, "What was it like acting with Mr. Shatner?" The first word out of Brian's mouth was "intimidating." He went on to say that it was like talking to a trial lawyer. Everything he said and did, Shatner reacted off of. This included facial expressions, body language, gestures, and tones. He said Shatner's focus was completely on him and he was in the moment. Then Brian stopped the conversation as only Brian could, and said he had to use the restroom and was done with this conversation.

When I got back on the plane back to Columbus, all I could think about was Shatner talking to the camera operator and Brian's experience acting with him. As I was looking out the small oval window on the plane and seeing the white puffy clouds, it hit me — Shatner's focus was off of himself, and that is how he "Smashed the Box!" Think about it — he was on a soundstage talking to Brian, and during their conversation he was aware of a camera operator moving his camera two feet.

From a strategic standpoint of "Smashing the Box," it allowed him to get out of the "Mental Prison" and in the present moment. That is the key; if we are to create, we must be in the present moment. This means being aware of our surroundings, the people we talk to, and everything going on around us.

Shatner not only reacted off of Brian's facial expressions, body language, and tone of voice, he also was completely aware of his surroundings. This is one of the reasons Shatner is able to improvise, be free, emotional, and spontaneous. The key to "Smashing the Box" is our ability to improvise. If we aren't able to be in the moment, we can't improvise.

Where is your focus during the day? Is it on the past, thinking about the future, or are you in the moment? In this day and age, I find being in the moment a rare commodity with distractions such as social media, blogs, TV, radio, podcasts, and advertisements. Ask yourself, how aware are you of your environment when you are in a conversation with someone? There is a direct correlation between our ability to improvise and our ability to shift the focus off of ourselves.

TECHNIQUE #2

EMBRACE MISTAKES

The Groundlings teaches its actors to embrace mistakes and allow ourselves to be imperfect. I saw an online video where Will Smith was talking to L.A. acting coach Aaron Speiser about a concept he labeled "Ruin the Take." Ruining the take is doing the opposite of what is written in the script. It is about experimentation, exploration, and embracing mistakes, which are key elements to the art of improvisation. For example, if the character is supposed to be sad, play him or her happy, if they want money, don't worry about money — you do the opposite of what is written.

"Ruining The Take" is a mindset that allows us to escape the "Mental Prison" and be free from the wall of perfection. I decided to ruin the take at one of my auditions for two reasons. One, I wanted to allow myself to make mistakes, and two, I wanted to reduce my fear and anxiety.

Before auditions, I would have full-blown panic attacks that crippled me and sabotaged my audition. One time, I was driving on Sunset Boulevard to an audition when an all-consuming panic attack set in. My hands felt like snowballs, my heart began pounding, and I began thinking negative thoughts. All I thought about was being terrible in the audition, never getting a call back from the casting director, and losing my agent.

When I arrived at my audition room, I saw 30 people who looked just like me: tall, skinny, white guys in their 20s with shiny black dress shoes. The number of people in the waiting room at auditions always intimidated me. I felt most of them were better than me and more talented.

Leaning back in my creaking chair, I looked around at the other actors and closed my eyes. At this point, the panic attack was full-blown and all I could think about was giving up my acting career. I didn't want to move back home since I loved L.A., my friends, the weather, and all the city had to offer. As my eyes drifted shut, I prayed to God and told him if he wanted me to leave L.A. and move back to Columbus, I would do it. I was done; I surrendered.

When I opened my eyes, what came into my head was "Ruin the Take." Was God giving me a message? Was he telling me to not be so hard on myself and allow imperfection, experimentation, and exploration to happen? This is where "Smash the Box" was born, in the waiting room of a casting office in LA. Once I allowed myself to "Ruin the Take," I tore down the wall of perfection, and my life would never be the same. I decided to give it a try in my audition by experimenting, exploring, and embracing mistakes.

As I opened my eyes, I watched countless actors enter and exit the audition room as I patiently waited for my turn. When my turn came, I got out of the chair and felt more relaxed than when I came in. My hands were still cold and my heart was racing, but the detrimental thoughts began to disappear. Going into the audition, I didn't feel I had to be perfect, and this freedom allowed me to gain confidence in myself and my creative capabilities.

As I entered the casting director's office, I handed her my headshot, went in front of the camera, and hit my mark, which is standing on the piece of tape on the floor marking where you need to stand for the camera. After I finished my audition, I shook the casting director's hand, exhaled, and left the room. On the way out of the room, the casting director said, "Good job." I nodded and left.

The first thing I noticed when I got in my car was how relaxed my body was. When I entered the audition room, I was tight, tense, and rigid from all the pressure I was putting on myself to be perfect and nail it. However, by changing my thinking and allowing myself to make mistakes, I felt less rigid and more loose.

After this audition, I used "Ruin the Take" over and over again, it was my go-to tool as an actor. When I landed a commercial with Procter and Gamble, it made me Screen Actors Guild eligible, which is a big deal for actors. For the audition I had a "don't care" attitude — I felt confident but not arrogant. All of this was possible by experimenting, exploring, and "Ruining the Take."

Are you a perfectionist? If so, do you allow yourself to experiment, explore, take risks, be wrong and make mistakes? Remember, allowing yourself to make mistakes isn't about sabotaging; rather the opposite, it is about experimenting, exploring, and creating. Without experimentation, exploration, and mistakes, we are prisoners to our mind and the wall of perfection.

TECHNIQUE #3

SAY "YES AND"

Saying "Yes And" is a fundamental principle taught at The Groundlings. Whatever your partner says to you in the moment, you accept it, build off it, and respond to it. In the simplest terms, you aren't saying "No" while you are on stage improvising. For example, if your acting partner asks you, "Why did you run from the police?", you would respond by saying, "Because I stole the money." You are accepting whatever they say as truth, building off it, and working as a team.

I remember doing an improvisational skit at The Groundlings that I struggled with. First of all, thinking on my feet is not a strong point for me. Second, I was in a class with great actors who were much more advanced and skilled than I was. Or, as you can tell, my wall of negativity was alive and present during my time in L.A.

On the first day of class, our instructor gave us an assignment to improvise that we were brushing our teeth. Simple enough, right? We had one week to work on this assignment, and I thought to myself what a joke, I don't need to practice brushing my teeth. I do it every night before bed, and this won't be an issue when I get in front of the class and reenact it. Sure enough, class comes around, and when it was my turn to improvise brushing my teeth, it was a disaster.

I didn't practice, and it showed. I pretended that I was looking into a mirror brushing my teeth, but all my actions were wrong. It didn't look like I was holding a toothbrush in my hand, but rather a baseball bat. Remember, I was miming my actions and didn't have an actual toothbrush in my hands. I was on stage moving my hands up and down, overacting the simple action of brushing my teeth. I also was a "No" person throughout my training, and I didn't even know it.

What I mean by that is my natural instincts were to say "No" to experimenting, exploring, and trying new things. We must not confuse being a "No" person with being a negative person; they are two different concepts. I am a positive person, however, I am not a "Yes And" person in life. I am hesitant to try new things, get out of my comfort zone, and break my daily patterns and routines. When I was doing this improvisational skit of brushing my teeth, I didn't do any experimenting or exploring. Rather, I simply got in front of the group and completely overacted.

I worked with The Groundlings for a few months and ended up quitting due to the struggle I was having with the art of improvisation. I could use the "Yes And" technique in the skits; however, thinking on my feet and making statements was very difficult for me. It is hard for me to make stuff up on the fly, be natural, funny, and in the moment. I gained a deep respect for sketch actors and performers, but I quickly learned that this was not my strong point.

Saying "Yes And" is the spark that keeps the creative process open and alive. It allows us to experiment and explore, try new things, and go into the unknown. What the Groundling's School of Improvisation taught me was that if we are to grow, take risks, and create, we must say "Yes And" on stage and off. If you want to put this principle to the test, watch an episode of "Saturday Night Live" and see how many times the actors say "No" to each other. The answer is going to be zero, because once we say no to people, opportunities and the creative process is shut down. We go into the "Mental Prison."

I did my signature keynote address "Smash the Box" for an insurance company in Cincinnati, Ohio, where I talked about the "Yes And" technique. I had two employees come up to perform an improvisational scene. Each employee was given a role: one was the boss and the other was the employee. The situation was the employee asking the boss for an extra week of vacation during the year. Both women needed to say "Yes And" to one another during the sketch.

The women's scene lasted a couple of minutes. They were able to create characters, a storyline and establish basic relationships. When it ended, I had them perform again, but this time I told them to say "No" to one another. This goes against everything taught at The Groundlings, but I wanted them to see the difference between using the "Yes And" technique and saying "No."

The sketch began with the employee entering the office and sitting down in the chair. The employee started to make her case on why she deserved an extra week of vacation time. The boss was on her computer typing, and when the employee finished her statements, the boss quietly turned to her and said, "No."

The employee pleaded her case on why she and other employees deserved extra time. She talked about the extra hours they put in, how they don't take lunch, and the incredible value they provide for the company. The boss listened, then said they can't do it at this time and she's sorry. The employee got up and walked out. The scene was over in less than a minute. This is what saying "No" does; it doesn't allow characters to be created, stories to unfold, or relationships to grow. In short, saying "No" kills the creative process.

A month later, I received an email from the woman playing the employee in the scene. In the email, she said being in human resources requires her to say "No" all the time to employee requests. She told me she was a "No" person and had to deliver this on a daily basis, and there was no getting around it, being in human resources.

She said she went back and looked at her old emails and saw they all started off with the word "No" or "No" was in the first sentence. She told me for one week she made a conscious effort to use the "Yes And" technique in her emails when she was talking to fellow employees. Her emails would go something like this: "Yes" I understand what you are asking "And" here is what we can do…

By changing the language of her emails, the woman said her mood changed. She said her job still had a lot of stress, struggles, and difficulties; however, by using this technique, she felt more open to possibilities as they arose. Think about that for a second — using the "Yes And" technique changed this woman's mood. I find it powerful to think that by changing our words from "No" to "Yes And" we can change our mood, create storylines, and strengthen relationships. This is what the "Yes And" technique is all about; it keeps the creative process open, alive, vibrant and moving forward.

Are you a "Yes And" person or a "No" person most of the time? This is a very important question we need to ask ourselves, and the answer will have a great impact on our ability to "Smash the Box." Of all the principles taught at The Groundlings, this is the foundation from which they teach improvisation.

TECHNIQUE #4

MAKE STATEMENTS

The Groundlings also taught us to "Make Statements." I know for many us this seems counterintuitive. We are all conditioned to ask questions. Yet, this is exactly what we must do if we want to improvise, get off the script of life, and "Smash the Box."

Again, watch an episode of "Saturday Night Live" and see how many times the sketch actors ask each other questions; you will hear some, but not many. Then, listen and see how many statements the actors are using throughout their skit, and you will see that the latter is the dominant form of communication.

I remember doing my first group improvisation at The Groundlings and, again, I struggled. I got paired up with a skilled improviser whose name was Bridgette. Bridgette and I were given a scenario where she was a protestor and I was a cop patrolling the rally.

I started the skit by going up to Bridgette and asking a barrage of questions. I asked her "What are you doing here? Why are you here? What is your problem? Why are you being loud?" I had a list of questions and fired off one after another until she got exhausted and the instructor stopped the scene. This is where she introduced me to the concept of making statements. The instructor said only asking questions in a scene does three things:

1. It doesn't move the story forward.
2. It doesn't create characters.
3. It doesn't strengthen relationships.

In my group improvisation, I didn't move the story forward, I created a shallow character, and I had no relationship with my scene partner. My questions kept the story stagnant; it didn't go anywhere, and it was boring to watch. I didn't have a character; I was just a cop who asked questions. There was no relationship between myself and my partner due to the clinical nature of my question-and-answer style. We did our skit for 90 seconds, and I couldn't tell you anything about my partner other than the few questions she answered. On a personal level, I didn't know anything about her.

In order for us to create stories, we must make statements in our personal and professional lives if we are going to create a story with a beginning, middle, and end. Relying strictly on questions generates cold and distant relationships, and I put this to a test when speaking with a group of realtors in Canal Winchester, Ohio.

While talking to the realtors, I told them the key to developing and strengthening relationships is making statements, not asking questions. I asked them whether they agreed with this concept of making statements? The majority of the members were nodding their head in agreement, but one man had his arms crossed and was shaking his head the opposite way. I had my focus off of myself and picked up on this man's nonverbal communication. I asked him why he disagreed with me on making statements.

He said in the real world of being a realtor, you only have so much time with your prospective client, and you need to ask as many questions as possible to get as much information as possible in a short amount of time. He went on to say that this sounds good in a classroom setting, but it wouldn't work in the real world. I turned to the audience and asked with a smile, "is my world not real?" I got a laugh, but I wanted to put his challenge to the test.

I asked the gentleman to come up on stage with me and to try one sketch where we were asking questions and one sketch where we were making statements to see what the different outcomes would be. He acted as the agent and I was the buyer in our role play. On the first tour, he was going to only ask questions.

He walked me into the pretend front door and began asking questions: Do you like the wooden floors? How about the space, is there enough space for you? Do you like the kitchen floors? How about the countertops? We made three stops during our improvisational scene in the living room, kitchen, and out to the backyard. Throughout the tour, he asked a number of questions, and made a few statements to gather the information he needed.

I told the man to go back through the house again, but this time to make as many statements as possible. He could still ask some questions, but should limit them.

At first, the agent struggled. He couldn't think of statements to say, so I helped him out by saying, "Oh, I love that the backyard is lined with trees." The agent then said yes, it gives you privacy and you have an acre of woods to enjoy as the homeowner. Next, we walked into the dining room and the agent said, "the wood floors are original to the house, they are 40-years-old." I bent down, touched the wood floors and told the agent that my wife would love them.

As we warmed up, he was making more and more statements about the kitchen. He commented that "the granite counter tops were made in Southeast Ohio and the cabinets are custom-made." I opened up one of the cabinets, checked the quality and agreed they were made by a master craftsman. Next, we headed into the entrance and the agent said, "Oh, and that door is a mid-century door that was made specifically for this house." I went over to the door, opened and closed it. I said, "I love it." We then exited the door and finished our scene.

I turned to the 10 agents in the room and said, "Who would you rather buy the house from, the agent who asked a lot of questions or the agent who made a lot of statements?" I didn't know what they would say, as I was making this exercise up on the spot. However, eight of the 10 agents said they would buy from the man who was making statements.

I then asked why. One of the agents raised his hand and said, "I don't like being asked a lot of questions," and all the other agents nodded their head in agreement. As I stood in front of the class, I was thinking the same thing; I hate being asked a lot of questions. I feel it puts me on the spot, I feel interrogated and, most importantly, I feel I am being sold to. I don't like the feeling of being sold to and often times when I feel this way, I shut down and end those conversations.

However, it also goes deeper than not liking questions when we did our improvisation. In order to create and innovate, we must reveal aspects of ourselves to others by making statements, which is essential to moving the story forward. When we rely strictly on questions, stories don't develop, nor do characters. Think back to our second sketch; I learned a lot more about the house and this agent when he was making statements.

He told me that I had an acre of woods that went with the house, the wood floors were original, the kitchen cabinets were custom-made, and the front door was from the mid-century. On the first go around, I didn't know any of this as I was always answering questions. In addition, on the second improvisation when he was making statements, the two of us had a couple of laughs and made a connection that wasn't there when we were doing a question-and-answer session.

I ended my keynote address with the agents by telling them a personal experience I had with an agent when I bought my house. I have bought one house in my life, and I remember talking to a number of agents during that sales process. However, the agent I ended up choosing made statements; she wasn't a question asker. She was eccentric and outgoing with a presence about her I loved.

I met her at the house I eventually bought in downtown Columbus. The home was in Shumacher Place adjacent to German Village. German Village is a historical district in downtown Columbus that has brick streets, slate roofs, and a grand park in the middle of the neighborhood. It is a highly desirable area and full of character, life, and charm. In short, German Village and Schumacher Place "Smash the Box" on the newer developments that are all one color and stoic in appearance and nature. I guess that is what drew me to the house and neighborhood; it was a unique neighborhood that didn't fit the mold.

When I saw the house, it was winter time and very snowy. I walked up to the front door and saw my agent looking through the front door window as I approached it. She opened the door and made a joke about the weather saying, "What a gorgeous day we have today." I laughed, dusted off my shoes, and entered the house for my tour.

The house was bank-owned and completely empty when I toured it. It was extremely cold inside, and I saw my breath in the living room. Throughout the tour, my agent made statement after statement regarding the house, saying things she liked about it and didn't like about it. Yes, she made statements about concerns she had for the house, which made me like her and the house even more.

I truly felt a relationship with the woman. I felt like I knew her as a person and an agent. She had a great personality, loved to joke around, and showed me sides of herself that few agents probably would ever show of themselves. But again, that is what "Smashing the Box" is all about. When we think, act, and operate differently, we will do what very few will do by being unique, original, and different. I was sold on my agent as much as the home, and eight years later I'm still there.

Are you more of a question asker, or do you make statements? We know we need to do both to be successful. However, if we strictly rely on asking questions, our ability to improvise is going to be short-circuited along with our ability to "Smash the Box." Remember, the greatest sketch actors in the world make statements to create characters, develop a story, and strengthen relationships. If we want to improvise successfully, we must make statements.

CHAPTER SUMMARY

How do you "Smash the Box?" By improvising — this is the key to the creative process that allows us to escape the "Mental Prison." The idea of improvising scares people, but we do it every day. Think of these four techniques as tools that can help you strengthen and improve your ability to improvise in your personal and professional lives. Imagine what your day would look like if you:

1. Got the Focus Off of You
2. Embraced Mistakes
3. Said "Yes And"
4. Made Statements

I know these four techniques work; I use them every day at work. They are truly a catalyst to help us get out of our heads, be in the moment, and allow us to begin "Smashing the Box."

In closing, watch an episode of "Saturday Night Live" this weekend and see how many times they say "No," ask questions, and cut each other off when they are talking. The answer to these questions will probably be zero; it won't happen. Now you have the techniques needed to go and "Smash the Box!"

Activity #1

DO
NOTHING

Activity #2

Are You a "Yes And" Person?

1. Are you open to new opportunities when they come your way?
2. Do you take risks?
3. Do you take chances?
4. Are you willing to break patterns and routines?
5. When someone brings forth a new idea or proposition are you open to it?
6. When you run meetings are your whiteboards clean or messy (see next section)?
7. Are you open to trying new things?
8. Do you like change?
9. Do you like taking a "leap of faith"?
10. Are you willing to get out of your comfort zone?

Total number of "Yes" answers: _____

Total number of "No" answers: _____

FREEDOM

ARE YOU IN OR OUT?

No one wants to live a life in prison, yet many of us do. Not physically, but mentally. We are prisoners in our own mind, trapped in our head. There are times we need to be in our head thinking, analyzing, reflecting on the past and planning for the future. However, there are also times we need to be present and in the moment if we want to create and innovate. Furthermore, there are distinct advantages to being out of the "Mental Prison" that affect our quality of life. Let us compare the differences of being in and out of the box.

IN

ANXIETY

I have had issues with anxiety most of my life. It runs in my family, and I accept it. I can't escape the fact that I have had panic attacks. I am always in a rush, and it is hard for me to slow down. However, I have awareness that when my anxiety levels increase, I am not in the moment but in the prison. Not only does the "Mental Prison" increase my anxiety levels, it creates an endless tape recorder in my mind that repeats a message over and over again, which exacerbates my stress levels.

For whatever reason, when I am in the prison of the mind, my thoughts replay themselves over and over again. Imagine playing a tape recorder and hearing the same message repeatedly. This is what happens to me when I am in my head thinking about the past or focusing on the future and not in the moment. Let me give you an example that has to do with me repeating numbers in my head.

I operate an acting studio called Broadway2LA. I have had the studio for eight years, and it has grown in numbers, but not in revenue. I have made a mistake over the years by not raising the cost of classes. Currently, I teach an eight-week acting course on Saturdays that includes a talent showcase where the actors perform for local talent agents and a casting director.

A great deal is involved in the eight weeks, and it should probably cost double what I charge. Over the years, I have been unable to pull the trigger on raising the rates, because I feared I would lose students and the enrollment would go down. Just the thought of raising the rates causes me an incredible amount of anxiety. I need that income to live on and, as I'm writing this, my wife is pregnant and we'll need even more money with a child.

Just like a tape recorder, I run this scenario of raising rates on my studio continuously in my head. The more it plays back in my mind, the more my anxiety levels increase. The numbers I am thinking about include raising my course rates by $25, $50 or $100; the higher I raise the rates in my mind, the more my anxiety levels increase. I constantly think about these numbers over and over again until finally a disruption in my day takes the focus off of me and my financial situation. The disruptor could be a phone call, a client, or an email that allows me to pause the fictional tape recorder and get back into the moment. Again, being in the moment is the key to escaping the "Mental Prison."

The "Mental Prison" also causes inaction. When we are trapped in the "Mental Prison," we rarely take action; rather, we think about doing something instead of doing it. Do you know people who talk a big game, who say they are going to do all these amazing things, but when it comes down to it they do nothing? These are individuals who are trapped in the "Mental Prison" and don't even know it.

The "Mental Prison" is a metaphor, but similar to a real prison, the goal is to keep the prisoner restricted, contained, and inactive. Imagine a prison where the prisoners had freedom, could take action, and produce results on their own. It doesn't exist, and it is the same with the "Mental Prison."

It wants us to be anxious, uncomfortable and not in the moment. This is our enemy. It wants to keep us out of the moment and in our head to retain its power over us. It controls our thoughts, feelings, and actions. It has total control. The less we are in the moment and the more we are in our head, the more power it has and the more power it wants.

OUT

CONFIDENT

When I am out of the "Mental Prison," I am confident, a risk-taker, and a dreamer. Knowing that I have permission to make mistakes increases my confidence level and allows me to do things other speakers can't do because of their wall of perfection. The last thing I want to do as a speaker is restrict myself with rules and regulations. I want to give myself the space and freedom to improvise and "Smash the Box."

Recently, I presented "Smash the Box" to 600 students in Hoover, Alabama. Before I took the stage, I told myself that I could be imperfect, make mistakes, and take risks. Giving myself permission to make mistakes is the catalyst for my creative capabilities; it takes the pressure off and allows me to perform up to my peak ability.

"Ruining the Take" increases my confidence to speak in front of groups because I know other speakers don't give themselves that freedom. They are operating with a tight filter. They don't allow themselves to make mistakes, and it shows in their rigid delivery. Speakers who are afraid to improvise, deviate from the script, or do something spontaneous or unplanned often times come off rehearsed and predictable.

I want to operate the opposite way. I want to be loose in my delivery, and be spontaneous and completely unpredictable with my audience. Speakers who try to be perfect can't improvise because they could make mistakes and go off "script." This is exactly what I want to do. I want to get off the script to be different, original, entertaining, and engaging.

And this is what I did in Hoover. When I went on stage, I shouted, "O-H," and you could hear a pin drop. Anyone living in Ohio would have said "I-O" to finish off the cheer used at Ohio State University football games, "O-H, I-O." However, being in 'Bama country, there was only silence. All the students in Hoover gave me a hard time for being from Ohio. Yet it allowed me to break the ice with them and have some fun. It was also an unplanned bit. It wasn't something written down in my outline or part of my regular address. It was a spontaneous and free moment, which is how I like to operate.

Mentally allowing myself the opportunity to make mistakes gives me the freedom and confidence to do crazy cheers, interact with audiences, and make a fool of myself. "Smashing the Box" is just that; it breaks down the walls that keep us constrained, restricted, and out of the moment.

Now, with that said, I don't recommend going into the state of Alabama and doing an OSU football cheer. However, hopefully you see the bigger picture. "Smashing the Box" gives us the freedom to do the unexpected. The freedom to take risks and chances that we normally wouldn't take. Risk-taking, doing the unexpected, and taking chances are all tied to confidence. Confident people can do these things, while unconfident people can't.

The question for readers is to assess where your confidence level is in regard to public speaking. Can you deviate from a script by taking risks and chances? If the answer is "No," more than likely you are operating from the wall of perfection and in the "Mental Prison." Remember, I am not asking you to be like me as a speaker; you need to be true to yourself and your style of speaking. I am asking you to give yourself freedom to experiment, explore, and create when you speak.

IN

EMOTIONALLY SHUT DOWN

When I am in the "Mental Prison," I am held captive to my emotions. I don't feel anything and am shut down. I go through life wearing a mask with a smile, while underneath the mask is sadness, anger, and frustration. It is a miserable feeling to be disconnected from my feelings and being in the "Mental Prison." It robs all of us of our humanity.

I learned in my training as an actor that there are five basic emotions all of us should feel on a daily basis. They are:

1. Happy
2. Sad
3. Angry
4. Fear
5. Loving

I went into acting to feel feelings. In particular I wanted to experience sadness, anger, and love. I didn't really know that at the time I decided to major in theater, but in retrospect it makes sense. To have an open invitation to feel feelings that I normally wouldn't feel during my lifetime energized and excited me. I got the opportunity to play characters I had never considered. They were inappropriate, vulgar, grotesque, and much different than the character I was in life — the real me.

One of the first characters I played was Tom Wingfield in the *The Glass Menagerie* by Tennessee Williams. In the play, Tom's father leaves his family at an early age, so Tom had to provide for his mother and sister. He always wanted to be a playwright, but due to his circumstances, he couldn't leave his hometown of St. Louis, Missouri. He had to support his mother and sister. He worked in a warehouse with fluorescent tube lighting, and he hated every minute of it.

There is a scene in the play I loved to act out, where Tom gets in an argument with his mom and they begin yelling at each other. I never yell in real life, and to have an opportunity to let it all out felt great. This particular scene is in the middle of the play, after Tom has come home very late from the bars and is intoxicated. He sees his mother as he stumbles into the house.

Once he closes the apartment door, she begins badgering him with a barrage of questions: Where have you been? Have you been drinking? How could you do this to your family? The last question is the one that gets under Tom's skin and sets him off: How can you be so selfish?

Tom explodes back at her and asks about all the sacrifices he makes for the family, such as giving up his hopes and dreams to provide for her and his sister. He gets face to face with his mother and points to a picture of his father who left the family when Tom was young. He says, "If I was selfish, I would be where he is, GONE." After saying this line, Tom storms out of the room and the scene ends.

Here is a man that works in a factory in order to provide for his mom and sister, and his mother is calling him selfish. As an actor playing this part, it wasn't hard for me to connect to his anger. Tom was never able to pursue his dreams and live the life he wanted to live. That is why I felt so deeply for this character. I was able to pursue my dreams by moving to L.A. and seeking a career in acting. I gave it a shot and I have no regrets, but Tom wasn't as fortunate.

Of all the roles I have ever played, Tom was my favorite. When I played him, I felt alive and energized. The word *alive* may surprise you; however, for me, that is what I felt when I played this character. To have the opportunity to yell and scream at my mom in the scene made me feel human and connected to an emotion I had suppressed for many years — anger.

By experiencing and expressing anger in this scene, I was out of the "Mental Prison," and I loved it. My blood was pumping, I had energy, and I felt alive. I had not expressed a lot of emotions in my early 20s, especially anger. To reconnect to my emotions in a healthy and productive manner was priceless to me as a person and an actor.

When we are in the "Mental Prison," it wants us not to feel feelings, it censors us and restricts us. That is why I fell in love with the craft of acting. I was uncensored and not restricted on what I could feel. Acting allowed me to break out of the prison by feeling feelings I had never felt before. Do you feel the five basic emotions mentioned earlier on a daily basis?

If the answer is "No" or you feel some of these emotions but not all of them, then your mind is holding you captive. We need to feel these emotions on a daily basis if we want to reconnect to our true selves and begin feeling human again. Remember the "Mental Prison" tells us that certain feelings are bad and that we should censor ourselves by staying in control. There comes a time in life that we need to forget about keeping ourselves under control and begin experiencing and expressing our emotions in a healthy and productive manner. This is what "Smashing the Box" is all about.

OUT

EMOTIONAL FREEDOM

When I am out of the "Mental Prison," I am alive; I experience and express emotions on a daily basis. The craft of acting has done a lot for me as a person. The most important lesson was how to reconnect with my feelings. Only when we feel feelings and express them are we truly alive and able to create. Creativity hinges on our ability to experience and express emotions on a regular basis. If individuals struggle with experiencing and expressing emotions, it will have a direct impact on their ability to be creative.

I remember a tear coming down my face in one of my acting classes in L.A. I had been training for over a year when I received a scene where my character was mourning the loss of a loved one. I was talking to my scene partner about my loss and, unexpectedly, the tear came out. When I got to the second page of the scene, more tears came down. It felt like boulders coming down a mountain. What a relief it was to me that I could actually cry.

I couldn't remember the last time I had cried, but it was probably at least 10 years before this. Imagine not crying for more than a decade and then feeling the sensation of a tear rolling down your cheek. I celebrated this moment, because it meant I had truly broken the "Mental Prison" by crying.

Emotional freedom is about feeling all five basic emotions in any order and in any fashion. You could even feel all five in one day if you are completely out of the "Mental Prison." My training in L.A. allowed me to escape the "Mental Prison," and I hope to never go back. I have my moments of being shut down emotionally, but they don't last long. I realize I am shutting myself down and that it is time to experience and express emotions.

What I have realized is that the key to escaping the "Mental Prison" is giving myself permission to experience and express feelings. Permission is key, and we all can do it; you don't have to be an actor to feel feelings. Somewhere in our adult life, we have been conditioned to think we don't have a right to express the five basic emotions. For me, it happened in high school where I told myself all I could be was happy and not experience or express anything else.

The result of only being able to express happiness was actually misery. It seemed like I was wearing a mask that had a happy smile on the outside, yet underneath the mask was a teenage boy who was anxious, lonely, and depressed. This is what happens when we shut ourselves down and restrict our emotional freedoms. As a result, I have gone the other direction in allowing myself to experience and express emotions daily.

I don't want to wear a mask anymore. I want to be free to say what I think and feel on a daily basis. This is why I began yelling in the car as a way to release stress and anxiety. I know it sounds crazy, but it is cathartic for me. It allows me to release all the suppressed emotions that I feel while driving. I got this crazy idea from tennis great John McEnroe.

During a tennis match broadcast, McEnroe was asked about his famous yelling rants on the court. He said it was a way to release stress, and it allowed him to perform up to his peak ability. If you think about it, keeping all that energy locked inside doesn't seem healthy or natural.

I know for me, once I yell and let out all my pent-up energy, I feel better mentally and emotionally. There is something cathartic about yelling and getting things off of our chests. Think about kids. They are always screaming and venting as a means of releasing energy and emotions. Again, sometime in our adult life we have restricted ourselves (notice a recurring theme here — restriction) from yelling and venting, and that is what puts us into the "Mental Prison."

Are you free emotionally? Could you yell when driving your car, regardless of onlookers? If not, give it a try once and see how it feels to "Smash the Box."

IN

PLAYING IT SAFE

The "Mental Prison" doesn't want us to take risks or chances. Rather, it wants to hold us hostage and keep us confined. Again, think back to the key message of "Smashing the Box" — improvisation. Improvising is about taking risks and doing the unexpected in a way that lies outside the four walls of prison. The "Mental Prison" uses fear as a tool to keep us inside our own minds.

When I am controlled by fear, I don't take risks. I stay in the "Mental Prison." One risk I have taken is investing in the stock market. Yes, a theater major investing in stocks is truly "Smashing the Box." I understand individuals and families' investment risk varies greatly, and for many this is not a suitable investment choice. However, if we only want to play it safe and risk very little, no great returns will follow.

I began investing in the stock market when I was a kid after my dad introduced it to me. When I was in L.A. waiting tables and living paycheck to paycheck, I quickly realized that if I ever wanted to generate income, I would need to invest in the market. This is when I began studying the market, the sectors, and individual stocks.

As you read about stock returns, keep in mind, I do like to gamble and take risks. By no means should you use my past performance as a guide for your investing. The point I am making is that the "Mental Prison" wants to keep us boxed, and this is my outlet for taking risks. You may find a different venue to do the same thing.

Incredible returns and wealth creation do not happen when we put our money in a bank account. I invest in the biotechnology sector of the market, which is considered very risky. Biotech stocks are biopharmaceutical companies that generally trade with high degree of volatility. Many biotech companies discover new drugs that have to go through trials before being approved.

In order to get a drug approved by the Food and Drug Administration (FDA), a biotech company needs to complete three successful trials with three phases. If these trials are safe and effective, they can send the drug for approval to the FDA. If unsuccessful, the company needs to run more trials and provide more data in order to file for a new review.

When a biotechnology company has a drug approved, the stock could shoot up in value. If it gets rejected, the stock price will plummet. I've had wins and losses investing in the stock market and, in particular, the biotech sector. One of my successful picks was a company called Human Genome Sciences (HGSI), where I bought 1,000 shares at $2.15 per share. They had a successful Phase III result with a drug for lupus, and the stock shot up to $34 a share. I sold the stock and made over a $30,000 profit.

One of my worst stock picks was a company called Delcath Systems, Inc. (DCTH). I purchased over 1,000 shares at $9.04 per share. They had an unsuccessful Phase III result for a chemotherapy drug system, and stock plummeted to under $1 a share. I sold the stock and lost over $8,000 on one trade.

I want to make money, and playing it safe isn't going to do it for me. I don't want to put my money in a bank account and receive less than 2 percent annually on it. I want to get a 35 percent return on my investment. Playing it safe limits our downside risk, but also our upside risk.

I love the stock market for the upside potential. The idea of investing in a company and making money off of it excites me. Again, "SMASH THE BOX" isn't about investing in this biotech sector — it's a mindset. It's about increasing our risk tolerance, allowing ourselves to make mistakes, and operating in a risky environment.

I look at investing from a different perspective. I believe I can make money by investing in stocks, while many people believe they can lose money in the market. We are both right, but our mindsets are completely different. I want to operate from a place of confidence and risk-taking. Those who avoid the market are operating out of fear and trapped in the "Mental Prison."

Do you play it safe? Do you allow yourself to take risks, and chances?

OUT

PLAYING FAST

Once we leave the four walls of the "Mental Prison" we are FREE, FREE, and FREE. Freedom gives us the space to try new things, do the unexpected, and take risks while experimenting and exploring. Freedom lies on the other side of the prison. When we escape, we can begin to live up to our creative capabilities and reach our ultimate potential by allowing ourselves to make mistakes and fail.

When you embrace failure, you give yourself a chance to do great things. This way of thinking applies in all aspects of one's life: social, personal, and professional. Kenny "The Jet" Smith while calling an NCAA basketball game once said, "you have to give yourself a chance to fail." He was referring to a star player who started out cold and, as a result, attempted too few shots in a game his team lost. Failure isn't anyone's goal, of course, but it's an inescapable potential consequence of trying to do really well.

A coach I have a lot of respect for is Pete Carroll of the Seattle Seahawks. Carroll talks about his players "playing fast." It means they are in the moment, reacting, and not thinking about making mistakes or being wrong. If a defensive back gets beat on a route, he has to get it out of his mind and prepare for the next play. Playing fast means you aren't worried about the last play, the last defeat, or rejection. Instead you are preparing for the next challenge that comes your way. We all have faced rejection, but the question is, do we beat ourselves up and wallow in it, or move on to the next play or moment?

When Carroll coached at the University of Southern California, I loved watching his teams prepare for games because of the confidence and bravado they displayed. Once before a game with Notre Dame, it was raining and his team was on a Slip 'n Slide having fun. Across the field on the other sideline, Notre Dame players were going through the traditional pre-game rituals like stretching and light wind sprints.

Notre Dame was in the "box" by doing the same pre-game ritual that every team does before games. USC was "Smashing the Box" by trying something different and improvising. "Smashing the Box" is about a mindset where one can experiment, explore, and try new things. In this particular case, USC was trying new things and Notre Dame was doing things the way they have always been done.

A fan might have said Carroll was crazy to let his players horse around before a big game, but it was the opposite. His "play fast" slogan included being loose before a game so a player could perform up to their true ability. That is what playing fast does; it keeps us out of the "Mental Prison" by not focusing on mistakes and keeping us in the moment. It takes the pressure off of individuals by allowing them to move on to the next play and not dwell on the past.

Let us all keep in mind that football is a sport, although some regions of the country act like it's a religion. With that said, having tens of thousands of fans watching you live and on TV creates a pressure-packed situation. Taking the pressure off prior to the game is a great tool used by Pete Carroll and was shown to be effective on the field later that day when USC defeated Notre Dame.

No one would question his team's tenacity, toughness, or attention to details if they watched USC's games and the amount of victories they piled up over the years. Carroll "Smashed the Box" with his coaching style, and the results included seven Pac-12 Championships and two national titles. He then returned to the NFL after a failed stint with the New England Patriots and won Super Bowl LXVII as coach of the Seahawks.

To be fair, he had a lot of talent at USC and in Seattle, but his ability to change mindsets and try new things allowed his teams to play up to their full potential. There are a lot of teams that have talent in the NCAA and the NFL that don't live up to it. However, that can't be said for Pete Carroll's teams in both arenas.

In short, all we can ask of ourselves and others is that we perform up to our full God-given potential, and playing fast can help us do that. We must live in the present and move on to the next play or moment if we want to play fast.

IN

OUT OF THE MOMENT

The "Mental Prison" keeps us captive by making us over-think and over-analyze situations. The more we analyze and dissect situations and circumstances, the more we focus on the past and think about the future. We stop living in the immediate moment.

When I'm not in the moment with acting, it's a disaster. The more I analyze a script and plan things out, the worse my performance becomes. Analysis truly leads to paralysis for me when I act, because I'm not being spontaneous and believable in the moment.

While at the University of Kentucky, I got cast in a play called *Wedding Band* in the lead role of Herman. It was my first and last main stage role I ever received due to my performance. To be in a main stage play at the University of Kentucky with a lead role was a big accomplishment in my career. It was one I was really proud of. I began memorizing my lines, analyzing the script, planning my performance and putting in extra work immediately.

When the performances came, I acted out my plan which included saying all my lines perfectly, making sure the audience could see and hear me, playing my character's wants and needs, and performing my actions on stage truthfully. Technically, I did a good job with my performance. Yet, in my heart I knew something was missing. I felt disconnected from my character and, more importantly, I felt depressed and defeated playing this role.

As each rehearsal went on, I felt more and more entrenched and captive. I couldn't get out of my head. I wasn't having fun. I was trying to be perfect with my performance and I was over-analyzing all of my actions. Picture a cold, gray, isolated prison, and that's how I felt in this performance. When I walked out on stage, I felt alone. There was an audience, but I was in my own little world. I knew my portrayal of Herman was ineffective and my negative thinking was about to come true.

After opening weekend, I read my first review in the local newspaper, the *Lexington Herald*. I opened up the Arts section of the paper to see a picture of the cast, including me. It was a great sight. Unfortunately, my smile dissipated quickly.

The review was negative on the show and on my performance in particular. It said I didn't deliver a believable performance as Herman. I was heartbroken. I shared the news with a fellow actor in the play, Bill, whom I had a lot of respect for. Bill received a great review, and I told him how disappointed in myself I was. He said it was one person's opinion and not to base my work off of it. I knew the review was correct, though.

The biggest problem in my performance was my inability to get out of the "Mental Prison" and be in the moment. I felt paralyzed on stage due to my need to over-analyze the script, my actions, and my thoughts. While playing Herman on stage, I thought about how I looked, how I sounded, and what I was doing. I was analyzing everything I was doing while I was doing it. This was a low point in my acting career, and one I don't like to remember.

Do you over-analyze situations? Do you live and operate in the moment? Over-analyzing keeps us captive in the "Mental Prison" and out of the present moment.

OUT

Being in the Moment

On the other side of the prison's walls is the unique ability to be in the moment. Being in the moment is a catalyst to the creative process. It allows us to be spontaneous, emotional, alive, and vibrant. Even more, it allows us to be aware of our surroundings and truly take in all that matters in life and our beautiful surroundings.

When we are in the "Mental Prison," we are held captive physically and mentally. The connection between our mind and our body is amazing. I know when I am in the "Mental Prison" that my body is tense and rigid. I can always tell in my back. Whenever I have back problems, I know I'm under a lot of stress and allowing myself to be in the "Mental Prison." I am analyzing everything and either focusing on the past or thinking about the future and not the present moment. This is the key issue — I am not in the moment. I am reflecting on the past or thinking about the future. When we put ourselves in the moment, it is our opportunity to escape prison and create.

I tried to escape the "Mental Prison" when I went for a jog on a Monday afternoon near my house in downtown Columbus. As I was stretching and getting ready for my jog, I realized how little I am actually in the moment. As I started running, I forced myself to focus on my surroundings and not think about the past or the future. Every two minutes, I would think about the future like my upcoming trip to Florida and the marketing campaign for my acting studio. However, I returned my focus quickly to my jog and my surroundings.

I live in a historical district that has a lot of character. It features brick streets, old houses with slate roofs, gas lamps for lights and a grand park in the center of the neighborhood. During my run, I noticed a house that had sculpted bushes in the front yard with an art deco design. The bushes started at the house and came down to the front of the sidewalk where they intersected to make the letter "V." Each bush was the same width and height. They matched perfectly all the way down to the front of the yard.

On the next block, I noticed one of the streets had rows and rows of trees with white flowers that were starting to bloom. As I ran under the trees, some of the petals were falling off, and you wouldn't know whether it was snow or leaves. As I turned the corner and headed back to my house, I took one look back at the trees and the white petals that lined the brick streets.

As I finished my jog and was walking back to my house, I saw a groundhog in my backyard. I stopped at my front door and just looked at the groundhog who was unaware of my presence. He slowly made his way through my yard and went under my neighbor's fence before vanishing.

I jog in my neighborhood two to three times a week in the spring and summer. I never notice these details or any others usually on my runs. The only reason I noticed the bushes, trees, and groundhog that day was because I consciously focused on being in the moment. What this made me realize is how much in life I miss out on when I am with friends, family, co-workers and clients.

Many of my experiences are robbed of unique qualities, images, and colors due to my constant need to plan, strategize, and anticipate the future.

How observant are you? How much of your day are you focused on the past or thinking about the future? Think about the last time you were outside when you took a walk or went for a jog. How much detail do you remember?

CHAPTER SUMMARY

You decide whether you want to live your life in or out of the "Mental Prison."

In:

1. Anxiety
2. Emotionally Shut Down
3. Playing it Safe
4. Out of the Moment

Out:

1. Confidence
2. Emotional Freedom
3. Playing Fast
4. Being in the Moment

Why I Re-Wrote *Smash the Box*

I remember talking to my dad about the release of my book, *Smash the Box* at the kitchen table in Zanesville, Ohio, about a year ago. I asked him what type of feedback he thought I would receive on it after it was launched. He sat back in his chair and softly said, "If people don't like it they won't say anything, and if they like it you will hear from them."

When I wrote *Smash the Box*, it was the first book I had written, and we took chances on it. Pages are out of order, it has no table of contents and even a couple of pages are upside down. We purposefully wrote the book to "Smash" the way books are written.

I love the creativity we did with the book. However, being honest with myself, I know I could have written a better book. Even more interesting, over the past year I have given out numerous copies and sold some with companies where I make talks having purchased a fair share. I have received very little feedback and it, to me, it reaffirms my father's statement that if people don't like it, they won't say anything.

What I have realized in life is that, generally speaking, the majority of people we come in contact with aren't going to tell us things we don't want to hear. How often have you told a friend or a spouse they are making a mistake on an investment, or changing careers is not a good move, or the vacation you have planned is out of budget? We must learn to differentiate truth from negativity.

We have confused being honest with being negative, and they are two different entities. Negativity is complaining, wishing for something better, being envious and seeing the bad in all situations. While being honest is giving someone constructive criticism as a way to get better, improve, and change. At the very least, being honest allows someone to know your true point of view regarding the issue at hand. We must decide to stay quiet and not say anything as a means of not hurting someone's feelings or tell the truth and give that person our honest point of view.

Activity #1

Yell Like John McEnroe

"Yeah, Yeah" Exercise*

Instructions:

Find a safe and quiet location (park, basement, open field, back yard etc.) where you can you do the "Yeah, Yeah" exercise. Once you have a location, follow these instructions:

Step #1: Crouch down and softly say, "Yeah, Yeah" a few times.

Step #2: Still crouching down but slowly starting to rise, raise your voice as you are saying, "Yeah, Yeah."

Step #3: As you are halfway up, continue saying "Yeah, Yeah" in an even louder voice.

Step #4: When you are totally upright, say "Yeah, Yeah" as loud as you can.

Step #5: Begin putting your body behind your words as you yell "Yeah, Yeah."

*Exercise created by Eric Morris, *Being & Doing: A Workbook for Actors*

Activity #2

Draw Your Prison/Burn Your Prison

Instructions — Draw Your Prison:

What does your "Mental Prison" look like?

Supplies:

- One sheet of paper
- Colored pencils or crayons

On a sheet of paper, draw your "Mental Prison." What does it look like? How big is it? What colors are in it? Next to the prison, draw yourself.

Instructions — Burn Your Prison:

Instead of taking your pictures to a licensed professional and analyzing your drawings, take a lighter and burn it. If you don't want to burn the paper or you don't have a lighter, you can bury it in the back yard or tear it up. The purpose here is to experience the relief of escaping the "Mental Prison."

BONUS

MATERIAL

Blogs

I wanted to give the readers four excerpts from my weekly blog that tie directly into the theme of *Smash the Box*. Each excerpt chosen ties into one of the four techniques we discussed on how to "Smash the Box."

1. Get the focus off of you — Blog #1
2. Embrace mistakes — Blog #2
3. Say "Yes And" — Blog #3
4. Make statements — Blog #4

If you want to escape the "Mental Prison," use these techniques and experience what it is like to be out of your head. Enjoy the blogs.

Blog Entry #1:

Silence

Why can't we be silent during a conversation? Because we feel we must always be talking or asking questions to keep the conversation moving forward. We are always anticipating what we are going to say next, which keeps us from being silent. Therefore, we become engaged in an endless stream of dialogue where both parties never stop to think, absorb or process what is being said. So, the goal in our conversations is to talk, ask questions, and avoid silence.

However, by avoiding silence we don't allow ourselves or the person we are talking to the opportunity to:

- Think — Silence gives you a moment to think about what is being said
- Reflect — Silence allows you to reflect on your answer rather than responding emotionally and impulsively

- Absorb — Silence allows you to absorb the information and content being delivered

Next time you are in a conversation, see how many silent pauses you or the person you are talking to have during your discussion. If the answer is zero, ask yourself what did you get out of that conversation? Were you able to think, reflect, and absorb what was being communicated?

As a speaker, I have been trained to pause throughout my keynote addresses when talking to groups and organizations. Professional speakers say audiences must have time to think, reflect and absorb when we are talking; otherwise the information will never be processed.

How many conversations do you have where information is never processed?

Blog Entry #2:

"Kick Out the Ladder"

Soichoro Honda, founder of the Honda Motor Company, personally experienced numerous crises and unexpected setbacks in his early years in the auto industry, such as a factory destroyed by fire, supplies rationed during wartime, and design fails that threw production schedules into a panic.

While the crises weren't welcomed, Honda began to note how each situation improved the eventual outcome. Over time, Honda came to value uncertainty as a catalyst for breakthroughs. Eventually he implemented a management practice that became known as "Kick Out the Ladder."

Just as a team neared completion on a project, he would create a crisis that would threaten everything. For example, if a team's deadline was eight weeks to finish a project, he would shorten the deadline to seven weeks. Creating this crisis forced his team to improvise and begin creating and innovating. He wanted his team to get away from thinking this is "how things have always been done" and think of new solutions, processes, and procedures.

Kicking out the ladder forces us to improvise and gets us out of our complacent state. Complacency allows us to coast through our days. It doesn't challenge us to come up with new ideas, practices, procedures or services. These things do not come from complacency, but from improvising.

What would happen if you kicked out the ladder?

*Excerpts taken from Erik Wahl's book *Un Think*

Blog Entry #3:

Messy Whiteboard vs. Clean Whiteboard

Mess is a composition of stuff, but it is also a vital part of the creative process. The creative process is a messy one in and of itself. It is writing, rewriting, brainstorming, erasing, and, finally, coming up with inspiration. Groups that make a mess on their whiteboard are much more likely to be creative than groups whose whiteboard is clean.

An organization with a messy whiteboard allows all ideas to be posted and discussed. It is not worried about limiting, censoring, or restricting ideas regardless of their logic or reasoning. Messy whiteboard organizations take pride in allowing all voices and ideas to be heard and posted so all feel part of the creative process. More importantly, messy whiteboard organizations know the key to creativity is planting seeds during meetings for innovation and inspiration. Innovative companies embrace crazy, audacious, and risky ideas and put them up on the board to be discussed at a later time.

An organization with a clean whiteboard allows only certain ideas to be posted and discussed. It limits, censors and restricts ideas as team members share them in meetings. Clean whiteboard companies take pride in discipline and censoring voices and ideas so only a few are part of the creative process. More importantly, clean whiteboard organizations value the status quo and keeping processes and procedures in place more than creativity and innovation. While ideas that are crazy, audacious, and risky are left off the board and replaced by ideas that are logical, linear, and safe.

What does your group's whiteboard look like?

Blog Entry #4:

Making Statements

The Groundlings School of Improvisation taught me to make statements. I personally love to ask questions, but this keeps me from thinking outside the box. Last week, I talked to a real estate company in Columbus and did my keynote address, "Eyes of a Leader." I had the entire audience perform improvisational games to experience the technique firsthand. Then I had one group come up and show their skits to the entire audience.

In the sketch, I had one woman be the real estate agent and the second woman be a potential buyer. The storyline had the agent showing the house to the potential buyer. During their scene, the agent walks the buyer through the home and makes statements about the house, which included how beautiful the kitchen is, backyard, and the foyer. Throughout the tour, she is sharing things about herself and the home to the buyer and establishing a bond between the two. The skit ends as they exit the house and get in their cars to drive off. During the skit both women talked, communicated, and established a connection the short time they were on stage.

After the skit, I asked the group what they thought about making statements, and I had one man raise his hand. He said, "In reality, when you meet a potential buyer you only have a very short time to work with them, and you need to ask as many questions as you can to get the information you need." He didn't agree with the value of making statements at a potential showing.

One of the women in the skit countered his statement by saying yes we have a limited time with the buyer, but how do you want to use your time? Do you want your showing to be filled with questions, or more of a conversation where both of you are contributing? That is what making statements does, it allows both people to share information with one another in a give-and-take manner.

I added to their discussion and said when I bought my house six years ago, the agent I chose had a great personality and didn't ask me a lot of questions. It's true, she shared a lot of information about her and I shared information about myself, and we clicked. I remember interviewing other agents and it was a question-and-answer period with all of them. I felt I didn't know who they were and they didn't know who I was.

In addition, I don't like being asked a lot of questions. I then turned to the group and asked them whether they liked being asked a multitude of questions in both their personal and professional life. All of them shook their head and said no. Even the gentleman who disagreed about the value of making statements agreed he didn't like being asked questions. However, he still felt it was imperative to ask questions at a future showing.

RESOURCES

"Smash the Box" Resources

1. Subscribe to Chad's Weekly Blog (Challenging conventional thinking) — www.chadjwillett.com

2. Chad J. Willett's YouTube Channel — www.youtube.com/chadjwillett

3. TEDTalks (Ideas worth spreading) — www.ted.com

4. SparkSpace (A cool and innovative place to spark new thinking) — www.sparkspace.com

5. IDEO (Design and consulting firm) — www.ideo.com

6. Freakanomics (Think like a freak) — www.freakonomics.com

7. Anthony Iannarino (The sales blog) — www.thesalesblog.com

8. Investment Research Dynamics (A cynical view of the U.S. economy) — www. investmentresearchdynamics.com

ACKNOWLEDG MENTS

Thank You, Thank You, Thank You

I want to thank my family, wife, friends and the Catholic Church who have all made this book possible. It starts with my parents, Lynn and Mary Kay Willett. You know love is unconditional when you tell your parents your sophomore year at the University of Kentucky that you want to be a theater major, and they still love you. I will forever be grateful to my parents who allowed me to dream, take chances, and live the life I wanted to live, not the life they wanted me to live.

Mary Kay is the inspiration for *Smash the Box*. She truly is one of the few people I have ever met in my lifetime who has lived her life outside the four walls of a box. Her endless love and belief in me as a person I will forever treasure.

Lynn is a father who has taught us all how to be people of integrity and dignity. My father is one of the smartest men I have ever known. He's always reading and thinking about things on a deeper level. He has shown me that no matter how you live, you can have a great impact on people's lives, something he has done in our family.

As for my brother, Jason, all I can say is "support." He was the best man at my wedding and I was honored to have him by my side. All of his friends and family will agree that if times ever get tough, this man will have your back.

My sister Allison has taught me the value of honesty, which resonates in this book. I have learned from her to say what I mean and mean what I say. When I came back from L.A. and lived in dishonesty and deceit, she called me out on it, and I will forever be grateful.

I would also like to thank my wife, Erika Castillo. What a blessing it is for me to have met the love of my life. She is the first woman I dated who I truly felt unconditional love from, and I am forever blessed. I have always heard that behind every great man is a great woman, but never understood it. Well I know I am far from great, but I am improved and a lot of the credit goes to this woman. I have so much love and respect for her and how she lives her life. I can't thank the Lord enough for meeting her.

I also want to say thanks to Mike, my brother-in-law, and Jennifer, my sister-in-law. Mike has taught our family how to enjoy the moment. He has taught me to treasure each moment you have with loved ones and never to take that for granted. Jennifer brings a non-judgmental attitude that I admire to the family. As long as I have known her, never have I heard her say something bad about someone or judge another person.

Finally, I want to thank the Catholic Church, the lord and our savior Jesus Christ. Jesus is our savior and I am forever grateful and humbled by his presence and unending love for all of us. If one wants to transform his or her life, going to church will do it. There is no magic "pill" or prescription that can change a person; however, having faith can change one's character. I always remember these seven words:

ALL THINGS ARE POSSIBLE THROUGH JESUS CHRIST!

I know you stopped reading at this point!!!

It's okay, I understand.

Meet Chad

Chad J. Willett (MA/BA/SAG/AFTRA) is a member of the prestigious Screen Actors Guild, successful entrepreneur, speaker, author, and creative expert. He specializes in creativity and innovation in regard to transforming cultures, redefining creative leadership practices, and working and living in the moment. His book *Smash the Box* purposefully SMASHES the way books are written with pages out of order, no table of contents, no page numbers and other elements.

After graduating with a theater degree from the University of Kentucky, he moved to Los Angeles to pursue his dream of becoming a professional actor. Chad spent seven years in L.A. as a professional actor (SAG/AFTRA member) where he was featured in the hit films *She's All That* with Freddie Prince Jr., *Halloween H2O* with Jamie Lee Curtis and *Can't Hardly Wait* with Jennifer Love Hewitt.

On the corporate side, he has worked for three Fortune 500 companies; Manpower, ITT Technical Institute, and *The Washington Post*. As an entrepreneur, he is the owner/operator of Broadway2LA Acting Studio. Currently, he resides in Columbus, Ohio, where he teaches classes at his acting studio.

Chad is a member of St. Mary's Church in German Village, Ohio, and the creator of "Make Faith Matter." He has also been involved with Big Brothers, Big Sisters and a reading literacy program for adults.

CPSIA information can be obtained
at www.ICGtesting.com
Printed in the USA
JSHW052248170123
36254JS00004B/20